I thought ... the world!

Recollections of life in rural Lincolnshire.

by

Kay M. Doak

Cover by Roy Hubbard

Published by
Hendon Publishing Co. Ltd.,
Hendon Mill, Nelson, Lancashire.

Printed by
Turner and Earnshaw Limited,
Sycamore Avenue, Burnley, Lancashire.

Contents

Acknowledgements

My first and most important acknowledgement goes to my husband, James, without whose love, encouragement and support this book would never have been written.

Next I wish to thank the East Lindsey Marsh Villages Society, which so kindly allowed me to use the material collected by two admirable ladies, June Houghton and Pat Hopper.

I would also like to thank all those people who agreed to be interviewed, gave so unstintingly of their time and made the interviewing such a pleasure. I am grateful to the people who kindly loaned or gave me photographs.

Finally, I would like to thank the village of North Somercotes, where we lived for so many happy years. It was that village that aroused my curiosity and started me delving into the past.

Kay Doak. Louth 1990.

The author was born in Kent and came to live in Lincolnshire in 1973. She is married with two sons. She was fascinated by the remoteness of the area and the fact that there had been little change over the years. She has written articles for newspapers and magazines and has broadcast on local radio.

INTRODUCTION

Lincolnshire is, for the most part, an undiscovered county. The M1 hurries past it, taking travellers to the north or south. Only those who have connections with the R.A.F., a desire to see Lincoln Cathedral or are holidaying in Skegness or Mablethorpe, venture to turn east.

This is nothing new. History took a fleeting glance at Lincolnshire and for the most part, passed it by. The Romans came and marched on to the north. The Vikings raided, then traded and were absorbed into the vast marsh area, hence the many village names ending with 'thorpe' or 'by'. No great battles were fought over its rich agricultural lands, although it is rumoured that Cromwell came to Saltfleet. If he did, he failed to make his mark. No great landlord claimed estates for his family and when the railway started to explore the British countryside, it chose but few routes into Lincolnshire.

For centuries Lincolnshire remained undisturbed, creating its own culture and way of life. It was the Second World War that brought the greatest changes and forced contact between the marshland flanking the east coast and the rest of the country. Indeed, it wasn't until the great flood of 1953 that many people had even heard of the marshland of Lincolnshire.

It could be said that the Marshes remained 'behind the times' until jolted into the twentieth century in 1939. What follows is a picture of the simple, undisturbed rural life from the turn of the century, taken from the recollections of Lincolnshire marshfolk.

Kiddings work on the beach at North Somercotes, 1916.
Kiddings are hawthorn cuttings which are set into the sand to enable loose sand to pile up over them and create the dunes which protect the Marshes.

A view of the Lincolnshire Marshes.

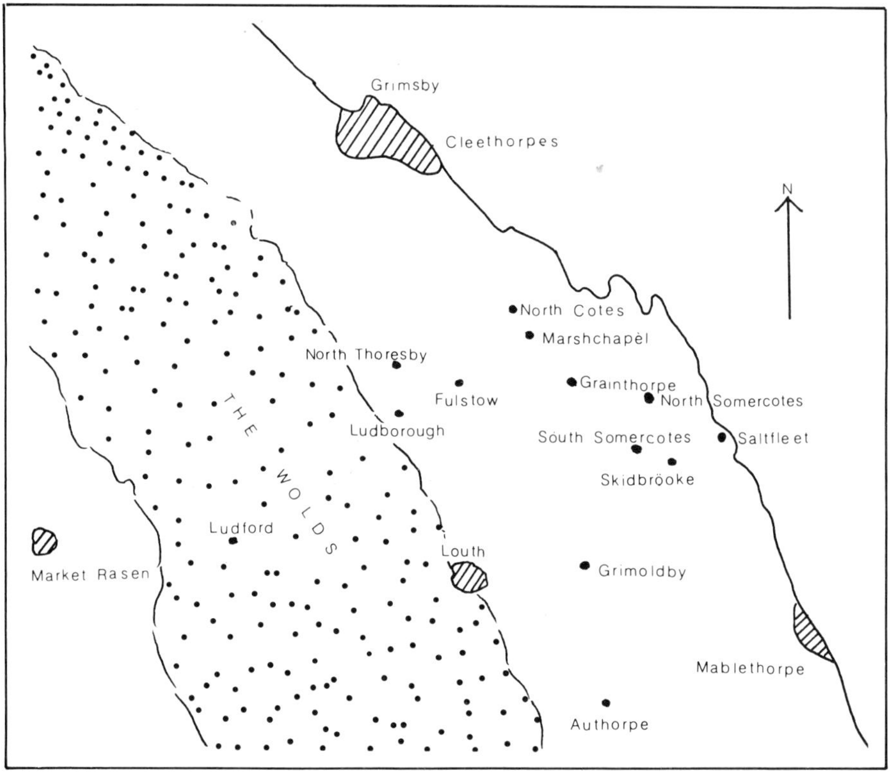

The 'Working' Farmer

To the east of Louth, which nestles at the foot of the Lincolnshire Wolds, are vast tracks of marshland. It is a fertile land covered by great open skies stretching to meet the North Sea. Possibly because it was a land that had to be drained and also faced the ravages of the east wind, no great landlord claimed it and it was left to be dyked and cultivated by small farmers. Certainly, at the turn of the century, it was a mass of tiny farms and small holdings and it was only with the coming of mechanisation that farms were amalgamated and large fields created.

This picture of the life of the small farmer is taken from the recollections of two farmers, born in 1905 and 1906 at Grainthorpe and Marshchapel.

Marsh farmers termed themselves 'working farmers', meaning that the owner worked alongside his men and didn't employ a foreman as many Wolds' farmers did. Possibly because the farmer shared the lot of his men, for the most part, his employees were contented. But perhaps, because they were so remote, they 'knew no different'!

The farms were mixed holdings relying on pigs, milk and crops for a living. 'We did rotation crops. Wheat, potatoes, barley and oats. We sold our corn at Louth Cornmarket and took samples in little sacks and got the best price we could. All the merchants had their stands round the wall.' Sadly, the site of Louth Cornmarket has become the home of the Halifax Building Society. The Victorian facade has been lost and only the weatherbeaten statue of Ceres remains as a monument to the labour of generations of farmers.

It was hard work with very little mechanisation. The sail reaper was drawn by horses but 'the bundles were tied by hand and stacked in stooks. Stacks stood for three to four months before thrashing'. In 1915 the first self binder came to the marsh. 'It saved a lot of work!'

All the ploughing and harvesting was done by teams of horses and the horses were all important on the farm. 'You worked all hours in those days if you worked with horses. You couldn't eat until you'd suppered up the horses. I worked from 5.00 in the morning and sometimes finished milking the cows by storm lantern.' This was on a farm of approximately 50 acres where 'father kept two good horses'.

Pigs were very important in marsh farming. The pig was the main stay of the labourer's diet and a pig was often given as part of the yearly wage.

'Farmers bought piglets at eight weeks and you turned your money over in three months. Pigs were fed on anything, swill, table leftovers, vegetable peelings. We gave them washing up water (there were no detergents in those days) and any waste coal there was, they did well on a bit of coal! I remember

The farmer's residence.

Lincoln Red cattle on a Grainthorpe farm today.

a farmer at Skidbrooke buying some pigs for eight shillings and we all laughed, they were a poor lot. But he fed them straight from the (milk) separator and some weeks later he asked me over to look at them. I couldn't believe they were the same pigs.'

Cattle were kept for beef and milk, but most of the milk was turned into butter. On the smaller farms, even if beef cattle were kept, they went to market. 'We never tasted much beef, even though we grew it!' Only on the larger farms where it could be afforded, did the butcher call with a piece of beef. Any other meat was home grown. 'We had everything else, vegetables, eggs, chickens and we killed our own pig.'

Some milk was taken round the village in churns and measured out with a ladle, there was no bulk collection as we have today. The rest was churned into butter by the farmer's wife or a female farm servant.

'In the summer months my wife used to make forty pounds of butter some weeks. She used to be up early in hot weather to churn it or it stayed soft. She used to put the cream in the spring trough to keep it cool.' Springs and wells were the only water supply on the marsh. A few pounds of butter were sold to a 'chosen few' in the village and some went to the village shop to be exchanged for groceries. The bulk went to Grimsby by carrier's cart to be sold to shop keepers or in the markets, the carrier returning with the money. Local butter was still sold or exchanged in the village shop during the Second World War. In 1937 the price of butter was 1/- (5p) to 1/6d (7½p) per pound and the butter money was the housekeeping for the farm.

Both farmers started work on their fathers' farms. One at the early age of 12 in 1917 because his father's man 'was fetched to the war. So I was taken out of school to work on the farm and I never went back'.

The other started in 1920 aged 14. Both agreed they were never paid. 'I never saw any money, I was fed and clothed but father put money in the bank for me. I never knew what I was worth until I got married.' (In 1927 aged 22).

'I started by mucking out the cows but I wasn't paid. Mother used to let me have something.' This was considered normal and not resented.

Life was comfortable in the Lincolnshire farmhouse. For the most part they were red brick under a tile or slate roof. There were three or four bedrooms but no bathroom and an earth closet down the garden. Downstairs, there was a front or best room, a living/kitchen, a scullery with a copper and sometimes a dairy room. Depending on the size of the farm, a maid or farm servant would have lived in. On most marsh farms employees had tiny tied cottages, as opposed to the bigger Wolds' farms where servants lodged with the foreman and his family.

The farmhouses were well furnished. Bedrooms had iron or brass beds with feather mattresses, rugs on the floor, swing mirrors, chests of drawers

A typical Marsh farmhouse at Grainthorpe.

The sty for the invaluable pig at a farm in South Somercotes.

and servant's boxes. The front room had comfortable chairs, a sofa and an organ or piano for mother to play. The kitchen had a scrubbed deal table and black-leaded cooking range with an oven and a water tank, to provide hot water for cooking and washing. The ceiling would hold the hooks from which the hams would be hung after pig killing. The scullery housed the brick copper, tub and dolly peg and most houses had a pantry where food was stored.

Most small farmers employed a maid or female farm servant, usually a young girl who had just left school and who stayed until she married. In nearly all cases, the maid was treated as 'one of the family' and helped the farmer's wife with general duties around the house and looked after the children. It was only in larger establishments that the distinction of servant was made and the young girl would have been expected to wear a uniform. 'The maid was like an older sister and took me for walks.'

Apart from working horses the small farmers had a pony and trap for shopping trips to Louth. One farmer could remember going with his mother to Louth as a small boy (in about 1912) and leaving the pony at the Temperance Hotel in Eastgate, Louth (now the site of Grandways supermarket). There the pony would be fed and tended by the ostler until it was required for the homeward trip. The pony and trap was also used for the annual outing to Cleethorpes. The farmer and his family went in the trap, the labourers and their families in the waggons.

The general picture was of a hard working family where even the children helped around the farm. But there was warmth, plenty to eat and an air of contentment with one's lot. It was thought that the farm labourers felt the same.

The Labourer

Waggoner, Gath Man, Shepherd

The lot of the farm labourer depended entirely on the farmer he worked for and whether he could specialise. These reminiscences have been collected from the residents of the marsh villages born between the years 1896 to 1914. They all worked on the land or were in service to small farmers during their working lives and they came from labouring families.

In the 1920s the hiring fair was still in existence in Louth for those who had not engaged for another year's work on 6th April, known as 'Flittin' Day'. The 'May Week' or 'May Wednesday' fair was held on the first Wednesday on or after 14th May and was traditionally the time when waggoners changed jobs if they were not satisfied with the position they held. About this time men would be heard asking each other, 'Are you stopping on then?'

A waggoner, who would wear a 'piece of horse ribbon' in his button hole to denote his trade, could command 39/-, a gath man (garth or cow man) with a 'corn dolly' 38/- and a shepherd with a 'piece of wool' 37/-. But a boy of 15, (in 1920 at Authorpe) who was just a general hand was engaged at £24.00 for the year, to live in and with no extra 'bargaining'.

Row of labourers cottages at Marshchapel (now demolished).

The labourers either had tied cottages or paid a very low rent for their cottage. Again it depended on the farmer they worked for. During the First World War a Marshchapel farmer paid 11/- (55p) per week, plus a cottage, a 30st. pig, 50 st. of flour, potatoes and kindling for the fire and the labourer 'saved money out of that'! But a labourer who worked at Wold Newton said with passion 'never trust a farmer to give you anything!' Money was deducted from the meagre wage to pay for the 30st. pig (30st. was the recognised weight for a fattened pig) and 'you had to bargain for fifteen faggots' (ash faggots cut from fencing stakes).

The cottages were of a similar pattern. Single Lincolnshire 'half houses' or in terraces of four or six. They were two rooms up and two rooms down with an earth closet, no running water and no electricity. It is hardly surprising that a row of cottages in Marshchapel rejoiced in the name, 'Shitt'n Alley!' But how another row came to be known as 'Tickle Cock Alley' the elderly resident could not remember, or was not telling!

The earth closets were remembered with a mixture of mirth and horror. One lady could remember 'falling in the bucket' as a child. While another shuddered and recounted 'it was creepy at night with the rats flying about'.

The privy at the end of the garden, which was 'creepy' at night!

One of the last 'Mud and Stud' cottages being dismantled.
The mud walls have been bricked over. Note the remains of thatch underneath the tin roof.

North Somercotes 'half house' demolished 1982.

But all the houses were remembered with affection and all said they were warm and cosy. Some were of 'mud and stud' construction with thick walls and a thatched roof. The design was generally to have a living/kitchen with a black-leaded range, some with over mantles. The back room was a small scullery for washing or pig killing and a walk-in pantry with a brick gantry for storing milk, meat and pork pies. The two bedrooms were reached usually by a straight ladder, sometimes a tiny staircase. The first room would have opened straight off the ladder and the second room led off the first. In families where there were many children, often the parents didn't sleep together, it being considered too dangerous for small children to be able to reach the ladder. Father slept in one room with the older boys and mother in the inner room with the girls and babies. In other families the larger room would have to be divided by a curtain to accommodate boys and girls sharing a room.

There was less furniture than in the farmers' houses and it was of a poorer quality. Some families slept on mattresses on the floor and the main furniture would have been a scrubbed table and wooden chairs, with a high-backed windsor chair for father. But again it depended on the generosity of the farmer in apportioning wages and bargains. One lady born in 1907, who was one of five, could remember beds with starched valances, white coverlets, servant's boxes, chintz covers on the chairs and starched net curtains. Her father was a labourer for a farmer in Marshchapel and her mother went out cleaning.

Food was plentiful for the farm worker albeit a bit monotonous. Bacon was the main stay of the diet, especially if it was part of the wage. The pig, when killed, was cut into ham and joints and salted. Sausages and pork pies were made and stored. Bacon would have been eaten at least twice a day. A farm labourer who lived in and was fed by the foreman's wife on a farm at Authorpe in 1920 recounted his daily diet. Cold bacon for breakfast at 6.30 a.m. Bacon and bread for lunch between 9 and 10 a.m. Cooked bacon and vegetables for dinner at about 3.00 p.m. and, if he was lucky and the foreman's wife was generous, some bread and milk was put in the oven for supper. If not, it was wait for cold bacon again at 6.30 the following morning. He shared a room with six other men and slept in a double bed with a waggoner. The only furniture in the room was the personal box belonging to each man. At another farm where he worked the bedroom had a concrete floor with no covering. The men washed outside at the pump and only occasionally got a stand up wash in a zinc bath of warm water. There was no heating in the winter and it was bitterly cold. He caught 'flu and the doctor insisted on the room being heated. A paraffin stove was supplied but taken away when he recovered.

Labourers in tied cottages fared much better. They were warm and much

Grainthorpe 'half house' demolished 1985.

Lincolnshire small-holders cottage at Grainthorpe.
It would have had a few acres and a tiny orchard. (Listed Grade II and for sale).

more comfortable. Most grew their own vegetables and soft fruits and often bred rabbits to supplement their diet. One lady recalled trying to keep pet rabbits when a child, but they 'disappeared, if there was nothing else for dinner!'

In most labouring families mother went out to work for at least part of the time, either on the land or cleaning for farmer's wives. Just after the turn of the century, women's wages averaged about 8/- (40p) a week for field work. By the 1920s they had risen to 2/6d (12½p) per day for potato picking from 8.00 a.m. to 4.00 p.m.

For the children, the choice of work was limited. The boys went into farm work or were apprenticed to allied trades, like the carpenter, the blacksmith and the wheelwright or to the local butcher or baker. For the girls there was field work or service. One lady told wistfully how she would have liked to train as a nurse but 'there was no opportunity'. The nearest hospital was eighteen miles away in Grimsby.

Children left school when they were needed to earn money. All had started work by the age of fourteen. The boys mostly followed their fathers into jobs. The girls often had to leave the village to find employment, but even at the tender age of fourteen they moved jobs until they found one they liked. One lady spoke of having several jobs until aged eighteen (in 1914) when she went to work for a farmer and stayed twelve years, although, when she started, he only paid 2/- (10p) a week.

Labourers at Sea Farm, Grainthorpe during the First World War.

Labourers at Sea Farm, Grainthorpe during the First World War.

A 'good horse' and farm boy, Sea Farm, Grainthorpe. Taken during the First World War.

Another lady, who was born in Grimoldby in 1898, went into service as under-house maid with a wealthy family who lived at Well House near Alford. This family had an indoor staff of eight, including a butler. During the summer the family went to Scotland for their annual holiday and the staff were taken to serve them. This was a great adventure for a farmer's daughter from the Lincolnshire marshes, for often, marsh folk didn't leave their villages for months on end, as will be seen in the chapter on entertainment.

A Marshchapel lady, ventured into Grimsby (eleven miles away) to find work. She had worked on a local farm for two years (1916-18 for £9 per year, aged 13) and left 'because she wouldn't give me any more money'. But she fared no better in the town, for her employer was very unkind to the two little country girls she employed. 'She nearly pined (starved) me to death. She used to lock up all the food and only left out bread and margarine for me and the other girl. They (the family) used to have their food in the room and if there was any left over, we could have it. We never got a sweet, there was never any left. I used to go to my auntie's in Grimsby for a meal!' This lady thankfully returned to work for a farmer in North Cotes where she was treated 'like family and used to sit with them in the evenings'.

Wages were very low for farm servants even though the purchasing power of the pound was far greater than it is today. But on the whole they were well fed and treated fairly. They worked very hard. In the words of one labourer, 'we knew no different!' Because the marsh people knew only low wages, the Depression years seem to have little impact on the area. However, farmers had more difficulty in selling their produce.

'Grimsby was hit by mass unemployment in 1926/7. We couldn't sell our potatoes and they stayed in the clamp until March. My father said he'd give me 2/- (10p) commission for every ton of potatoes I sold. (Potatoes usually sold for £2.00 per ton). I went to Grimsby because I wanted the money but I didn't sell one ton. I went to Mr Dickinson in Wellowgate and he said he'd like a ton but he just couldn't sell them. Grimsby was hit bad, so was Cleethorpes. They relied on the textile workers from Bradford coming for their holidays but they didn't come.'

However, all agreed no one on the Marsh went hungry and everyone had work of some kind. 'It didn't affect the working farmers so much because they were able to cut down on their expenses and they never took holidays.'

The general opinion was that, although many families could not afford luxuries and there was little to spare, as they grew their own food they had much to be thankful for.

Entertainment

Fairs and the 'Greasy Pole'

From the chapters on farm life and farm labourers, it would appear that Marsh life consisted of all work. To a large extent this was true. It must be remembered that there was little or no mechanisation. Electricity didn't come to the Marshes until the onset of World War Two. Horses were still in use until after the war and mains drainage and refuse collection were not known until the 1950s.

All household chores had to be done by hand. Water had to be fetched from a well or pump. There were no washing machines, spin driers or electric irons. Vacuum cleaners were unheard of until the 1950s and '60s and cooking was done on a coal-fired range. Food had to be kept on the cold shelf in the larder or in the spring trough, so it was necessary to bake and cook regularly as nothing could be put in a deep freeze or refrigerator.

The Marsh area also had a long tradition of Methodism and the work ethic was strong in most families. 'We knew nothing else,' admitted one labourer and an elderly lady when asked when she started work, replied, 'from the moment I left the cradle!' A farmer, when asked by his wife if he would like some slippers for Christmas replied, 'When should I wear them? I takes me boots off and I goes to bed!' All this meant that days off, outings and fairs were looked forward to with great excitement and were enjoyed to the utmost.

The two most important Fair days in Louth were 'May Wednesday' and 'Martinmas Fair' (23rd November). Villagers from all around went to these fairs, travelling by pony and trap, carrier's cart, waggons, bicycles or walking. In the words of a North Somercotes farmer, 'Apart from these two days, folks never left the village. From the Fish Shambles to Lloyds Bank, (Cornmarket, Mercer Row area of Louth) I have seen the streets so full that you could walk on peoples' heads!'

As well as the hiring fair in May and the produce stalls, there were skittles, coconut shies, roundabouts and side shows and the 'first Cake Walk and Aerial Chairs I ever saw'. It was a time to meet friends and for the young people to do a bit of courting. To 'get among the boys' as one lady put it. Young men liked to show off their skills at the rifle range. But they had to be careful of the 'sharp jacks'. 'They sold things that were no good and got you to bet on things that couldn't win. They stopped them from coming!' (Unfortunately, the elderly farmer never told us how that was achieved!)

Some villages had their own fairs. North Somercotes had swings and roundabouts in the yards of the Bay Horse and the Axe and Cleaver.

Outing to Donna Nook (dunes behind North Somercotes) taken in 1920s.

Marshchapel, for many years, had what was known as the Marshchapel Feast. This consisted of various types of races, a band and a picnic tea. In 1867 it even advertised Bear Baiting, but locals who could just remember the feast, for it died out soon after the turn of the century, seemed to think this was some sort of game and not the tormenting of a bear. However, many remembered the climbing of the greasy pole, or those who attempted it and failed. A flitch of ham or a leg of mutton was tied to a pole lathered in grease and the young men of the village tried to climb to the top to claim the prize. Those who tried had some very mucky clothes for their pains!

Saltfleet staged an important horse fair until after the Second World War, by which time it had become a mini agricultural show. Pigeon shoots were popular, even in thick fog as one was reported!

But the treat that was remembered with most affection was the Sunday School or Band of Hope outing. This took place in the summer usually between haymaking and harvest in early July. The farmers loaned their waggons and there was a prize for the best dressed horse and waggon. The outing was usually to the sea beyond North Cotes or to Donna Nook beyond North Somercotes and food was taken for the day. Sometimes the farmers donated the food for the children. The beaches here are very sandy and ideal for children to play and build sand-castles. But they are too dangerous for swimming. Some of the men would take out the Donna Nook lifeboat or

Saltfleet Horse Fair before First World War.

play quoits. The women would keep an eye on the children, whilst doing their knitting and chatting. It was a welcome rest from stacking stooks or tossing sheaves.

Sometimes the outing from Marshchapel and North Cotes was the long drive to Cleethorpes. It took two hours to reach by pony and cart and the first thing to be done on arrival was 'to have a meal!' as the party had probably set out at seven in the morning.

There was much more to see and do at Cleethorpes. There were stalls and side shows along the sea front and boat rides. All this made an impression on a little country boy of about seven or eight (1913). That little boy, now a retired farmer, remembered 'the man who had the boats had a big red nose and called out, "Come with me! Come with me!" But I never went!' He also remembered with much glee seeing two men fighting on the beach and having his first dodgem ride for 2d.

Those villages close to the railway line like Grimoldby and Saltfleetby had an even more exciting time on their outings, they went by train to Mablethorpe. It was probably the only time that the children went on the train unless they had family in Louth.

As 'nobody could afford much', entertainments were home made. The children played in the meadows, 'counting the wild flowers' and went round the village 'getting into mischief!' Skipping ropes, hoops and whips and tops were the favourite toys and one lady remembered when the nail wore down on their tops they would call into the cobbler's shop in Marshchapel and the cobbler would put in a new one.

As the children got older and reached their teens the amount of entertaiment they had depended on whether the family was strict Methodist or not. In strictly religious homes, dancing and going to the pub was forbidden and the young people had to be home early. But some houses had a piano or a gramophone and those families would have musical evenings with their friends.

Dances were held in some villages but many ladies said their fathers would not allow them to go. Those who did said they could remember dancing the lancers and on one occasion the dancing became so wild that one girl twirled so hard that she 'ended up sitting in the coal bucket beside the fire'. Music was provided by piano, violin, drums and cornet but often there were no refreshments and never any alcohol.

In Marshchapel, all the ladies agreed that women seldom went to the pubs with the men (most villages had more than one pub). The only women seen in the pubs were the wives of the Grimsby skippers who came with their husbands on an outing from the port. The Grimsby ladies were thought very fancy in their fox furs and large hats. The pubs catered for people coming by pony and trap or on bicycles, which were popular means of transport, and they served meat pies, potatoes and gravy. The men would play cards and dominoes. One lady who admitted going to the pubs with her parents assured us she only ever drank Oxo!

All the villagers agreed that life was very quiet in the Marshes and evenings were spent at home in the winter or tending the garden in the summer. They seemed to like it that way. One lady said that when she was taken to visit relations in Grimsby, she was quite frightened by 'all the traffic'. When all the traffic that passed through the village amounted to 'half a dozen carrier's carts going to Grimsby' or, 'the Post Office van and the Silver Queen bus', it is hardly surprising!

Outing to Cleethorpes 1920s.

Shops and Shopping

A little of anything have you thought of today, Ma'am?

Next to working, shopping was the most important part of village life. Most goods that were not grown, were purchased from the village shops, from travelling salesmen or through the offices of the carrier who brought goods from Louth and Grimsby. For the most part the village shops sold 'everything'. Groceries, household goods, clothes; these shops were Alladin's caves smelling of spices and polish and anything that could permeate through the fumes of the paraffin heaters and oil lamps. Not only was the village shop a source of merchandise and a means of communicating with the outside world through the Post Office or telegraph counter but it was where news was exchanged, gossip repeated and messages left if someone was sick and needed the doctor.

Marsh villages had to be self sufficient for they were all miles from the nearest town and perhaps one of the best examples is North Somercotes. Ten miles from Louth, eighteen from Grimsby and twelve from Mablethorpe and bordered by the North Sea, it was as far from civilisation as it was possible to get. The shops were general stores and North Somercotes always had at least two.

Brown's shop was remembered by all the elderly residents. The building is still there today but it has been turned into a private home. From before the turn of the century it had been a grocery shop and bakery and employed bakers, roundsmen and at least two girls, living in to serve in the shop.

In 1931 the wages were 10/- (50p) per week plus full board for a young girl straight from school. For this she would be expected to work from eight in the morning till eight at night every day except Wednesday, which was a half day and Saturday, when the shop was open until nine. There was very little free time and the only relaxation was, perhaps, a bike ride and chapel on Sunday. The girls had to be in bed by ten, but were provided with a comfortable chair to sit in to do sewing or embroidery in the evenings after work. One lady, who was in service there for ten years (1931 to 1941), remembered that her chair cost 4/6d (22½p) but it took her five years to embroider her table cloth because she had so little free time!

All the family worked hard in either the shop or the bakery and the girls were treated as family. The girls rose at seven thirty although the bakery staff had been hard at work for hours.

Breakfast consisted of bread, marmalade and tea. Sunday was the only day they had a cooked breakfast. Mid-morning there was Camp coffee and a bun from the bakery and someone left the shop during the morning to cook

Brown's bakery and general store, North Somercotes.

Roberts' grocery shop, North Somercotes. The small building on the right-hand side was where Miss Neilson had her hat shop.

lunch, which was always meat and vegetables and perhaps a milk pudding. Tea was at five o'clock and there was always tea and biscuits before going to bed.

This was true even through the Depression and during the Second World War. Country folk fared much better than those in the towns, because they grew their own vegetables, still made their own butter and cheese, reared chickens and tame rabbits and had the invaluable pig. People from Louth would go to the Marsh villages for functions like harvest supper, because they were sure of a good feed! Units of the Green Howards were stationed at North Somercotes during the war and the W.V.S. cooked for the soldiers on duty. Large tins of beans were supplied from Brown's shop.

Apart from being a bakery and selling groceries, the shop sold drapery and clothes, corn and household goods. Delivery boys were employed to take out orders, first on bikes or with a pony and trap and later, by van. It was a much appreciated service for isolated farms.

It is interesting to recall some of the prices in the 1930s. A large loaf was 3½d (approx. 1p), buns seven for 6d (2½p), Woodbines 3½d for 10 cigarettes. A pair of good quality sheets 5/11d (approx. 30p), a pair of pillowcases 2/- (10p), sugar 4½d (approx. 1½p) for 2lb and flour 7d (approx. 3p) for half a stone (7lb).

Fulstow Post Office and village store taken about the time of the First World War.

Goods were not packaged as they are today. Butter came in 56lb blocks and during the war years had to be cut into 2oz portions for rationing. Lard and margarine were cut into 4oz portions. However, most village families had pork dripping to fall back on when the ration ran out. Sugar was delivered from Grice's warehouse in Grimsby in one hundred weight sacks and had to be weighed into blue one pound and two pound bags.

The young girls who worked in the shop enjoyed being sent into the bakery because 'it was always warm in there' and sometimes it wasn't in the shop, especially in the depth of winter. But some of the bakers were known to be 'free with their hands!' Even years before, when ladies wore long skirts, small boys hung around outside the shop to tell these ladies if they had a floury hand print on their skirts. One elderly resident remembered earning 'many a penny from one lady in the village!'

North Somercotes, being one of the larger villages in the Marsh, had several shops. As far back as the 1851 census two draper/grocers were listed among the trades of the village. But smaller villages often had at least two shops and a Post Office. Marshchapel is a prime example.

Brown's rival in North Somercotes was Roberts' shop, still known as the village stores today although it only stocks a fraction of the merchandise that was available in Mr Roberts' time. The information about this shop came from a lady who had been apprenticed there from 1943 but many elderly residents confirmed that the shop had hardly changed since the turn of the century.

Roberts' shop was considered a high class grocery shop as the owner had been trained at Sainsburys and was a member of the Federation of Grocers Institute. The F.G.I. certificate was always prominently displayed in the shop window. Mr Roberts employed a manageress who was also a window dresser. The windows were dressed to a very high standard, one side of the shop displaying groceries, the other, drapery and clothes.

Young girls were apprenticed at the age of fourteen and worked from 9.00 a.m. to 5.00 p.m. for 10/- (50p) per week. (It is interesting to note that in 1910/12 women earned approx. 8/- (40p) per week for field work). At age sixteen, the hours went up to 8.30 a.m. to 6.00 p.m. and the wages went up accordingly. There was one half day off a week and an hour for lunch and half an hour for tea.

Mr Roberts was a very strict employer and insisted on a very high standard but many who worked for him said 'he was a good boss to work for.' However, he had his little foibles. He did not allow price tickets as he thought it defaced the goods. The staff were expected to memorise the prices for the goods and this wasn't easy when there were three different sizes of cocoa for example. He was fastidious about tidiness. All paper and boxes had to be cleared away and grocery orders had to be packed in the

Postcard of North Somercotes dating from about 1918.

The windmill has been demolished and the chapel is now a block of flats.

The Axe and Cleaver and the coal merchant, North Somercotes.

correct order. Blocks of soap and boxes of matches double wrapped at the bottom of the box. Tins placed in the corners and everything else packed in between finishing off with the fats, butter and lard and anything that might be squashed. The bill was made out and attached to the packet of tea. (He presumed that would be the first item required!) The orders were made up over night and the bills checked by Mr Roberts. Any mistakes had to be corrected the next morning and woe betide anyone whose order made the delivery late!

Roberts' shop had a wide range of goods apart from groceries and farm produce (butter was bought from selected farms and the farmers were paid in kind). The drapery department stocked curtain material, roller blinds, coconut matting, oil cloth and lino. There were men's trousers and jumpers, working boots, bib and brace overalls and blue working jackets known as 'Slyvers'. Thick collarless 'Union' shirts and thinner 'Oxford' shirts were also stocked. For ladies, there were dresses, shoes and corsets, taken home and tried 'on approval'. Part of the shop had haberdashery drawers for cotton, thread, elastic, pins, buttons and tape. The chemist's drawers, which were only removed in the 1970s, stocked all sorts of home remedies and the shop had a poison licence and a licence to sell methylated spirits and paraffin. With all these items under one roof one can imagine the smell of the shop!

The villages had all the trades connected with farming. Blacksmiths and wheelwrights, which in time gave way to the garage, windmills, many of which have been demolished, cobblers and saddlers, now only found in towns. Because of the close proximity to Grimsby, most of the larger Marsh villages had fish and chip shops. These have survived.

In the smallest villages, where there was perhaps only one shop the range of merchandise was limited so travelling salesmen called. Coalmen, butchers, bakers and milkmen had rounds as they still do today in rural areas. Firstly, with a pony and cart, then later in small vans. The delightful quote at the beginning of this chapter was used by Mr Dawson from Fulstow, who sold groceries. Other travelling salesmen remembered were the paraffin man and the man who sold pots and pans and brought them round the village in a basket on his head. He was especially remembered as he liked a drink in the village pub and one day after a particularly good drinking session, he and his basket of wares ended up in a dyke as he missed his footing on a dyke bridge. An elderly lady from Marshchapel remembered getting a smack from her mother for laughing at the poor man. Dykes or drains, as they are known in the Marsh, could be particularly smelly places! There were travelling tailors to villages where no tailor existed. North Somercotes' tailor had a room at one of the village pubs, which was considered good for business. At Marshchapel, they wished they had a travelling tailor, as many said their resident tailor's clothes were so awful they usually had to be re-made by the village seamstress. A Mr Cawkwell was the travelling tailor from Louth and in the 1920s he charged five guineas (£5.25) for a good quality suit.

Haberdashery salesmen and a china and crockery salesman were remembered and even an opium peddler whose half penny and farthing weights were the same! The salesman the children looked forward to was the man who sold oranges. These were a luxury to country folk and his arrival heralded Christmas.

Goods that couldn't be bought in the village were collected by the carrier from Louth or Grimsby. The carrier was an invaluable member of the community and will be covered in a later chapter.

Transport

Carrier, Bicycle or Shank's Pony.

As has been recounted in a previous chapter, to leave the village was a treat and some only left for the annual fairs. Farmers had ponies and small carts in which they went to market or their wives went to Louth for extra shopping, say at Christmas time. The only transport available to the labourer was a bicycle, if he had one, his own two feet, or if greater distances were involved, the carrier's cart.

The carrier was a valued member of society. He carried not only goods and people but news, gossip and was sometimes the only face that would visit an outlying farm in days. He travelled the countryside in a covered waggon bringing goods to the villages and taking produce to the markets and corn exchanges. Everyone interviewed remembered the carrier. Just prior to the First World War the only traffic on Eskholme Bend, now part of the A1031, 'would be half a dozen carrier's carts going to Grimsby'.

One lady remembered her first trip to Grimsby from Marshchapel (about twelve miles) when she was about nine years old (1908). She thought it was

Roberts' shop with the carrier's cart outside.
Note how the name of the street has changed. It has been known as Town Street, Front Street and finally Keeling Street.

wonderful but was rather frightened by all the people and carts. To get to Grimsby she met the carrier's cart about 5.00 a.m. and arrived at noon after all the stops and delivering. She and her mother had three hours with a relative then travelled back, arriving in the village well into the evening.

The carrier, Joe Blythe, was well remembered. 'You were longer on the road than you was in Louth. He would never run his horse. It was always on the trot and some man asked him if he couldn't go a bit faster and he said "If you want to go any faster, you can get out and walk!" '

The carrier could take six or eight people to Louth but a place had to be booked. It took three hours from Marshchapel and cost one shilling (5p). In the winter he gave passengers a blanket to wrap round their knees. It must have been freezing crossing the Marsh in January or February. Villagers would spend only a short time in Louth, then return in the late afternoon. A lady could remember going with her mother and having her dinner at the Pack Horse Pub in Louth. 'Meat and vegetables, 6d (2½ p) and milk pudding for the child, 1d.'

Carriers were often asked to bring items of clothing from Louth if the local shop could not supply what was needed. Several pairs of shoes would be brought from Stead and Simpson for villagers to try on and the money and the unsold shoes returned on the next journey. One lady told of a farmer who asked the carrier to buy "th' owd lass two nightgowns" from Godsmarks in Louth. When the carrier asked what size he was to bring, he was told, "Tell 'em it's for a twelve years old but she's a big lass for her age!"

Ladysmith Road, Grimsby 1910.
A far cry from the rows of labourers' cottages on the Marsh.

On their slow journeys some carriers liked a drink. Another lady told of the carrier who came back to the village a little merry after several stops on the way, wearing a lady's hat which had been ordered for a wedding.

To reach Grimsby from the northern end of the Marsh it was possible to go by train but this entailed a five mile walk to the station at North Thoresby unless a lift could be begged from a cart going that way. This too would have been a special day out and looked forward to for weeks.

By the 1920s the motor bus was taking over from the carrier and even today, it performs the function of the carrier. Parcels often arrive in Marsh villages courtesy of the local bus. During the First World War the first lorries came to the Marsh. They were chain driven and would sometimes take passengers to Grimsby. 'I remember my mother and sister going, their legs hanging down the back!'

Grayscroft Coaches ran north into the Marsh from Mablethorpe, started with 'gratuity money from the First World War'. The first coach was 'carpenter built with an engine inside it'. Another of the first bus services on the Marsh was run from North Somercotes by 'Clockie' Wardle. (He also repaired clocks!) The bus went from Somercotes to Grimsby and was called *The Violet.* Goods and chickens in crates would be tied to the top of the bus and it stopped at the White Hart in Grimsby, where goods were taken to the Corn Exchange for sale. Villagers could remember char-a-bancs with canvas seats round the sides and not being able to see out!

Another company was the Silver Queen. It ran from Louth to Grimsby and out to the Marsh via South Somercotes. The *Silver Queen* was open topped. 'I paid a shilling (5p) and nearly lost my hat at Ludborough!' The only company surviving today in the northern Marsh is Appleby's 'Pride of the Marsh'. It is interesting to note that some villages had six carriers a day before the First World War. Today, these services have disappeared and villages have no transport at all, except the private car.

Many had to rely on a bike or their own two feet to get them about. A bicycle was a treasured possession as it took a long time to save up the fifty shillings (£2.50) that a bike cost in the 1920s. If you had one, you got about and saw more, like the Louth flood in May 1920.

'Some lads came out from Louth (to Authorpe) and told us and we couldn't believe it. I got on my bike and rode in to see for myself.' There had been a cloud burst and water had poured down off Hubbard's Hills. 'Houses in Ramsgate were washed down.'

The last resort was walking. Children walked to school, sometimes a distance of four or five miles. If the weather was very bad, they 'didn't go, because we hadn't got mackintoshes'. Men walked miles to separated fields to work the land or out on to the grazing marshes to tend or collect stock. No wonder boots were so important as the next chapter will show.

Clothing and Wash Day

In country areas clothes had to be warm and serviceable and fashion was a secondary consideration. Because the Marsh area was so remote, fashions changed very slowly and adults clothes were often cut down for children, so some of the older styles remained for a very long time.

The most striking point that arose when any elderly villager talked about their clothing was the fact that no one wore shoes. Everyone, old or young, male or female, wore boots. They all spoke of hobnailed boots and the difficulties of using a button hook when they were young. One farmer remembered with pleasure his first pair of shoes. He was 22 and about to be married (in 1927). Boots were needed by the adults when working. Most children had to walk to school, sometimes quite a distance over muddy tracks or poor roads, shoes were useless. Boots were the most expensive item of clothing and difficult to afford in poorer families. In such families the child who was first to rise had the pick of the boots available and therefore, the most comfortable pair. The late risers got what was left, whether they fitted or not.

Consequently, the cobbler was an important member of the community. Every village had at least one. The cobbler in Marshchapel was a cripple and remembered with affection as he supplied nails for tops and the children would go into his shop to lift down the boxes of nails he couldn't reach. In North Somercotes, the cobbler's little wooden hut stood for many years in the corner of a garden, long after it had ceased to be used. One farmer remembered his father paying the cobbler annually, as was customary with farmers, a sum of £10 or £12 (in about 1912/14). This was a large sum of money from one family, but a year was a long time to wait for payment!

As has been stated in a previous chapter, the village store could supply most types of clothing or goods could be ordered from the carriers. However, a trip to Louth or Grimsby was a special treat and there was more selection from the larger shops. Lawson Stockdale, Stead and Simpson, Gale's and Godsmarks were the shops most frequently mentioned, not only for clothes and shoes but material for dressmaking. It is commonly thought that country people made most of their clothes but in the Marshes this is not true. There were a few women who made clothes for their families, but on the whole there 'just wasn't time' or 'mother had too many bairns to look after'. When one considers the lack of conveniences in the houses and the fact that many mothers had to do field work to supplement the meagre income, it is realised that only those whose husbands were working for a generous farmer, or who had small families, had time to sit and sew.

Most villages had what one farmer described as a 'village benefactor'. This was a lady, usually a widow, who was village seamstress. She would make and cut down clothes for a busy family. She also helped to nurse the sick, sat with the dying and helped to lay out the dead, as well as being on hand to 'get the pig away' (helping to make the pork pies and sausages). She was a self-appointed 'home help' and families paid her what they could afford. Wealthier families would employ her all day and give her meals as well. It was known that if the seamstress was given more than she could eat, she wrapped up what was left and took it home with her.

On the whole the clothes for women were of dark colours, black, navy or brown. Skirts were long and blouses and dresses had high necks. Coats with leg o' mutton sleeves were remembered even into the 1920s and only slowly was the fashion of calf-length skirts and bobbed hair adopted. There were no hairdressers and only North Somercotes laid claim to a barber. Hair was cut at home and ladies fashioned their hair with crimping irons and curling tongs. Many ladies remembered uncomfortable nights with rags in their hair to make it curl.

The material for clothes for the winter was a heavy worsted, although alpaca and cashmere were mentioned and one lady remembered having a velvet dress. She was an only child and her father had a small business in one of the villages. Check dresses seem to have been popular for school wear, always with the apron over the top. The boys wore knee length trousers and as many left school to start work aged 12 or 13 they wore them until they could fit into a pair of men's trousers.

Almost everyone interviewed said they had best clothes for Sunday school, chapel or special occasions. However, there were poor families where clothes had to be washed and dried by the fire on a Saturday, so as to be ready for Sunday morning. Those children did not come out to play on a Saturday.

Even wedding dresses had to be serviceable and capable of use on future occasions, so many ladies said they did not have a white wedding dress but one that was for best for years after. A typical example was 'a grey dress with a blue and brown hat' (1926).

Hats were worn much more than they are today, by both men and women. Ladies prized their hats and if they could not afford a new dress, a new hat was not always beyond their means. North Somercotes had its own hat shop. It was in a small building opposite the Woolpack pub. It opened two days a week. On other days the lady who lived in the thatched cottage next door (now demolished) had the key and would open up for customers to look round. The milliner was a Miss Neilson, who lived in Grimsby. She made hats to order or would cover buckram shapes with a piece of material to match a dress. A lady in North Somercotes remembered having a hat made to match her dress and buying a 'tam with a long plait of wool and pompoms'. In 1922 a good class hat cost 3/11d (just under 20p). 'For some that was a week's wage.' So Miss Neilson had cheaper hats costing 2/11d or less. She also re-trimmed hats with new ribbons and braid.

The men wore 'Union' shirts from the village shop, thick corduroy trousers and canvas leggings, 'to stop the mice running up their legs at harvest'. Even in summer, they seemed to retain their waistcoats and all wore a hat of some description.

As has been said, there were no washing machines and certainly no easy care fabrics as we have today. Washing for the family was an all day job and very hard work. All water had to be drawn from a spring, well or pump. Sometimes there was only one to a row of cottages, where you had to wait your turn with a bucket. Because families lived in such close proximity, wash days were often communal events. But, as in all communities, neighbours didn't always get on. Tempers flared in 'Shitt'n Alley' and two women ended up hurling cabbages and throwing water over one another!

Some cottages had a scullery with a copper heated by coal. Others were too small and clothes had to be boiled in a bucket over the kitchen range. This gave rise to the cold meal on wash days because mother was too busy with the washing and the range was fully occupied with washing buckets. Clothes were washed in a wooden tub with a dolly peg and put through the mangle if one was owned or shared with a neighbour. The early mangles were heavy and not easy to use. Sheets were wrapped round a roller and a box of stones or heavy weights dragged across to press out the water. When the clothes were dry they were pressed with a flat iron on a thick pad on the kitchen table and aired round the fire. The irons ranged in several sizes and had to be kept clean with a bath brick. They had other uses too. A lady spoke of her Saturday morning job which was to iron the stair carpet through thick brown paper to melt off the drips of wax from the candles that lit the children to bed.

Pillars in Society

The Marsh had no large landowners or aristocracy. The only important people were the doctor, clergymen and schoolmaster and a few of the larger farmers, who were generous to the poor.

As is the case today, the doctor lived in North Somercotes. It was central to the northern Marsh and the largest village. Two houses were used by doctors in North Somercotes at various times. They were Sycamore House and Victoria (now Somercotes) House. Today, there is a modern health centre and Somercotes House is the home of the dentist.

All the villagers remembered the doctors. Dr Collingridge, Dr Lockheed and Dr Gabby, who practised in Somercotes at various times and Dr Higgins in Louth. They were remembered visiting on horseback or by pony and trap but 'you couldn't afford to have 'im unless you was forced to'. 'If you couldn't afford to pay just then, you paid over a time.' There was no National Health scheme until after World War Two. If a villager could afford the doctor, "you have to find a way of getting 'im". There was no telephone and usually a message was left at the village shop or someone

Victoria House now Somercotes House, North Somercotes.
For many years the home of the doctor, now a dentist's surgery.

rode or walked to North Somercotes. One lady remembered her mother carrying her brother a distance of over two miles to the village shop to await the doctor, who called there. The child had a temperature of 103 degrees and after he was treated he had to be carried home again (1920s).

Many children died in infancy and much illness went untreated. Ladies spoke of having severe headaches, nose bleeds and fainting fits. Most villagers admitted 'mother did all the doctoring. The doctor was only called when all else failed'. (Sometimes it was too late.) Home remedies like brimstone and treacle, liquorice powder and sweet nitre were used. One lady in Marshchapel spoke of having butter, sugar and vinegar heated on a stove by her grandmother as a remedy for a cold. In Louth, people went to a Mrs Jarvis who had a shop near the site of Louth swimming pool (Church Street). She dispensed herbal and home-made remedies for spots and cuts. Many people took their children to Mrs Jarvis when they were ill.

Life was very hard for anyone who had an accident. A lady told how her father was crippled when the granary platform collapsed when he was carrying 18st. (over two hundredweight) of wheat on his back. He never worked again and had to make a meagre living growing vegetables, tending the garden on his knees and breeding rabbits for the pot. His wife and children had to work to see that the family did not starve. However, the villages tried to 'look after their own'. There was a type of unofficial adoption, where families in work would take in a child from a poorer family and feed and clothe him until he could return to his own family. When a pig was killed needy families were always remembered and a portion would be given to one of the 'Parish Bread Monkeys'. (Someone receiving Parish relief.)

A lady from Marshchapel spoke of her grandfather, who was on crutches. 'The cup of his hip was gone. He went to Hull (Infirmary) but they couldn't do nothing like they can today.' However, there were successful operations and they were great events. One lady spoke of a member of the family having a growth removed from his lip and another, of riding in the carrier's cart to Louth with her sister, who was going to have her tonsils removed.

Without a doubt there was poverty in the rural areas but all those who knew it spoke with great affection of the clergy. 'The parson was very good to poor people. He would help them buy boots for the family.' A lady who was born in Grimoldby spoke of the vicars being very good to the poor, of them lending money for people to get started in farming and even buying bicycles for 'deserving people' so that they could get to work more easily.

The parson at North Cotes, Parson Johnson, was known as a 'dear old man'. The vicarage had a lovely garden planted with shrubs and flowers and it was always open for villagers to stroll in after service on Sunday.

The majority of Marsh folk were Methodists and some families had a very strict code of conduct, even to making sure there were no newspapers in the house on a Sunday. Families went to chapel twice, sometimes three times, on a Sunday. But no one seemed to mind, except one lady said her 'young man' accompanied her once but wouldn't go again because 'it took too long'.

Everyone remembered Sunday school with great pleasure and not only for the treats and outings. One lady even recited a verse she had learned over eighty years ago.

Joy isn't a big word but it has a big meaning.
J is for Jesus, O is for others and Y is for yourself.

School was recalled with mixed feelings. The headmaster at Grainthorpe school, Mr Hatton, was looked upon with 'reverential fear' by one of his former pupils. Another lady who attended Marshchapel school said, 'I didn't like it. I wasn't keen at all. I disliked most things, except playtime!'

The education was very basic, reading, writing, simple arithmetic, some geography and history, sewing for the girls. In schools where there was land, gardening for the boys. But as most pupils left school from 12 years onwards in the early part of the century and at 14 up to the Second World War and there was often time off for potato picking, carrot pulling, caring for the younger members of the family, or just plain bad weather, there was little time or incentive to pursue a subject too deeply.

A few said they went to evening classes after they had left school but found it difficult to keep up. Most of the Victorian schools remain in the Marsh, albeit with modern additions, some as incongruous as a satellite dish!

Politics were important to the men as the small farmers were one of the last groups to get the vote. Several recalled elections and the excitement

National School, North Somercotes, built in 1854. Note the pump for drawing water.

there was before them. The baker at Marshchapel, Mr Wray, was known for his 'politicking'. He was a strong Radical and would start a discussion on the doorstep whilst selling bread. He would then walk back to his cart and his customer would think the discussion was closed. But Mr Wray would think of some other line of persuasion and come back to start again. The bread was often late getting round the village!

Two little rhymes concerning the Louth constituency were repeated with glee about the election of 1910, where Mr Langton Brackenbury, Conservative, was opposed by Mr Timothy Davies, Radical.

Run away Timothy, run away do.
Your name is wrong for us, you see
It ought to be Langton Brackenbury.
We'll shout and storm
For tariff reform
And kick the damned Radical out!

However, from the other side came,

Timothy Davies in a motor car
His wife by his side.
Brackenbury in the swill tub
Calling for a ride!

Langton Brackenbury won the election in 1910 and remained Louth's M.P. until his death in 1920.

A class of North Somercotes pupils c. 1900.
The teacher William Taylor retired in 1939.

Momentous Events in the Marsh

The day the moon fell out the sky at Marshchapel

Life wasn't always humdrum in the Marsh and there were events in villager's lives apart from the two annual fairs and the Sunday school outings that they remembered as something special.

To all of them, Christmas was a time that merited individual mention because for many families, especially the farm labourers, it was the only time when presents were given. Birthdays were remembered but hardly ever celebrated as there was no money for presents. If mother was a good needle woman or was able to knit, socks, gloves or a new item of clothing would serve as a gift. Christmas was 'much thought on' and meant a holiday and a feast. Something different from the eternal pig meat!

Poultry was favourite for Christmas dinner. Turkey that was always 'very high' or rabbit, 'rabbit made us a good dinner'. If a labourer was employed by a generous farmer there might be a piece of beef. George Burgess was remembered on the Marsh for his generosity to the parish widows at Christmas time.

North Somercotes Sunday school outing to Mablethorpe 1921.

The poor looked forward to 'Mumpin' Day', the feast of St Thomas (21st December). That was the day when poor women and parish widows or one of their children, but never both, trimmed their bonnets and wore a clean white apron and visited the local farms. They were given money which they used to buy extra food for Christmas. A lady from Marshchapel said the money was usually spent in the village shop buying dried fruit for the Christmas pudding.

The houses were decorated with evergreen such as holly and mistletoe and possibly a small Christmas tree, 'mother always tried to have a little tree'. Most people remembered their Christmas stocking. It had an apple, orange, a few nuts and sweets, possibly a penny or small toy or something useful and home-made.

This is one lady's account of Christmas in 1924 when she was ten years old. 'The first Christmas I remember was the one when we went to Scunthorpe (by train from North Thoresby) to my father's brother. I got a black box with a brush, comb and mirror in it and a stocking with an apple, orange, nuts and a threepenny bit. I thought I'd got the world!'

The two World Wars made a tremendous impact on the Marsh villages. They brought strangers in the form of the soldiers, who were billeted in the villages. The wars took husbands and sons away. Some were never to return.

Possibly the First World War had the most impact. Farming wasn't a reserved occupation as it was in 1939 and able bodied men were 'fetched to war'. This left the farming to old men, women and boys. For some, the war was an excuse to get away from the drudgery of farm work and seek adventure. One young man who was an apprentice wheelwright at South Somercotes, 'didn't like his lodging', so he joined up when he was 18. He lost an eye on the Somme and found that war wasn't all glory and adventure. A lady spoke of her husband joining up at eighteen and 'drinking water that had had dead men in it'.

Farming itself was disrupted by having horses commandeered without warning. A farmer took a loaded wagon drawn by four horses to Ludborough station and returned with an empty wagon but only two horses to pull it, the army had claimed the other two.

In Marshchapel, some soldiers were billeted in the Wesleyan Sunday school building but there were few facilities for them, unlike the officers, who had better accommodation in Marshchapel Hall. 'They used to come round to mother's to have a wash and brush up before they went out.' Even to the country folk, who were used to hard work, the treatment of the soldiers at times seemed very harsh. They were made to march from Marshchapel to North Thoresby station (about five miles) in full kit (60lb approx.). 'They never sent any wagons for them, but the officers rode.' 'There was one officer, he was a sod to them men. The men said, wait 'till we get him across yonder, we'll have him! And they did. He was soon shot dead!'

The tranquillity of the countryside was shaken by the arrival of the Zeppelins and the bombs. Grimsby was bombed and a lady from Marshchapel, who was in service there, remembered the windows of the house being blown in. 'We went to look at the hole, you could have dropped a big house in it!'

The sight of the aeroplanes flying over the Marsh was awe inspiring, especially when aged four. One man could remember being carried out of bed by his mother to see them. When an aeroplane actually landed just outside Marshchapel, the villagers were terrified it was a German! However, it turned out to be a British pilot, who had run out of fuel. A young lad was sent to guard the plane and stop children playing with it or trying to take souvenirs. He was there such a long time that his mother took his dinner and a drink to him. Wars were not won on an empty stomach!

The horror of the war and the loathing of the Hun penetrated the Marsh area as it did all over the country. Peas named 'Prussian Blue' had to be fed to the pigs as no one would buy them.

The Second World War was not as devastating to the Marsh in as much as far fewer men were lost. Farmers stayed put and fought the war by feeding the nation. Soldiers were billeted in the villages again, to guard against invasion and the villagers helped to feed them. Many families took soldiers home for a meal on Sundays after chapel. Meat and vegetables were plentiful, only sugar and dried fruit were in short supply. The W.V.S. cooked for the soldiers on duty in North Somercotes. Soldiers going off duty in Grainthorpe hung around for early milking to be given a glass of milk straight from the cow.

Ladies in the villages formed knitting circles to knit socks, gloves and woollen helmets for the soldiers on guard on the beaches, where the cruel east wind could cut like a knife (and still does on occasions!). A.R.P. and Home Guard Units were formed but thankfully were never needed to fight an invasion. A few bombs fell on the Marsh and one or two villages were machine gunned. North Cotes was singled out for attention and the villagers took a very dim view of it, as it was 'Sunday afternoon!'

In the Second World War the Marsh came face to face with the enemy through prisoner of war and displaced persons camps. But the hatred never ran as deep as it did in the 1914 war and some of the inmates didn't return to Europe but married into Marsh families and stayed to farm the land.

The war was a time of enterprise for some in the Marshes. 'Men used to catch Pyewipes (Peewits) and send them down to London. They called the birds down and set trap nets to go over them.' But it was never discovered what the birds were sold as once they reached London!

For one or two Marsh folk there were events that stuck in their minds and were of great importance. Such as a lady from North Somercotes, who was in service to the vicar of Conisholme in the late twenties. She and the family were driven in an Austin Seven to North Cotes to see the Prince of Wales (later Edward VIII) arrive by plane. He was on his way to Grimsby to open the Corporation Bridge.

A farmer told of the first time he went droving. It was 1918 and he was 12 years of age. He and another lad, who was 'in khaki and had to salute an officer' drove twelve unbroken horses from Grainthorpe to Market Rasen (about 24 miles) and exchanged them for 'sixty-three beasts' (cattle). 'They were big too, some of them were two years old.' They stayed the night at Ludford on both journeys and on the return journey they stayed over night at Louth as well. He laughed as he remembered the trouble the cattle caused wandering off into private gardens and especially remembered them being chased out by a gardener from the garden of a large important house in St Mary's Lane, Louth.

Perhaps the most endearing story and the one which shows the solitude and remoteness of the Marsh is the story of 'the day the moon fell out the sky at Marshchapel' (in 1913).

A retired farmer, now in his eighties, told how he and a few friends were playing 'in the road, as usual, when we looked up and saw a white object floating in the sky. Well, we'd never seen anything like it. And someone said it was the moon coming down!' The children chased after the object, the farmer being looked after by his family's maid and one can imagine their wonderment as they watched a balloon come to earth between Marshchapel and North Cotes. Not only was this an awe inspiring occasion but the pilot of the balloon spoke French! They must have thought it was the man in the moon as well. The villagers had to send to Grainthorpe, because the only person who spoke French was a young man called Sowby, home from school on his long summer holidays.

Marsh life was gentle and unhurried. It changed little over the decades. These chapters have only scratched the surface and given just a glimpse of what life was like. The people who lived there were hard working and undemanding. They never envied others because 'we knew no different' and most of them thought they 'had got the world'.